God revealed His majesty, wrapped it in His glory, and gave it to me in a package I least expected.

The true story of how my journey with breast cancer became a gift that changed my heart forever.

Anne, Survivor

I would like to dedicate this book to my family:

~First, to my daughter Emily, whose gentle spirit reflects the true face of God.

~My son, Paul, whose will power strengthens me and his gift of prayer humbles me.

~My son Erik, who defines what walking by faith really means.

~My best friend Bill, for being my anchor in the storm.

~My mother...I truly believe you are an angel living among us.

~Most of all, I would like to dedicate this book to our God, who IS the giver of all good gifts, and the Keeper of all His promises. Thank you for all you have given me.

TABLE of CONTENTS

It is with a humble heart that I find myself placing thoughts and words on paper, in hopes that someone, somewhere, may read them and be inspired. It is my hope that these words are not mine, but actually His, the author of life Himself. May our good and gracious God guide my thoughts, and may His words inspire. For I want my life to be about Him, His glory, His majesty. I have come to appreciate life as my journey has brought me to this place. My stories are more than stories about triumph. They are stories about hope...the hope that allows me to believe in a God who is bigger than life itself. It is within these stories that I find God's promises intertwined within my life. Embedded within these promises are God's embrace, God's love, and God's mercy. God promises life, not death. He promises never to leave us. God promises to be faithful. God is real because I have felt his touch and heard His voice. I have seen Him work through those people that have loved me in my darkest fear. When this happens, I get a small glimpse of His deep love for me. May my journey, written on the pages of this book, gift you with a yearning to seek His face and embrace His love. Blessings, Anne

"I am not afraid of storms for I am learning to sail my ship."

(Louisa May Alcott)

~One~

God's Provisions

"God promises peace to His people."
(Psalm 85:8)

As I began this journey, I started to rely on God's promises. The bible is rich with stories of Yahweh's provisions. I have learned that He is not only a God of the past, but is a God of the present, and will not stop being God in the future. I have learned to trust Him to be true to His word.

The bible depicts His faithfulness...I have experienced it.

The bible depicts His compassion... I have felt it.

The bible sings of His majesty... I have seen it.

The bible is written about His love... I have felt it.

I have read these stories, and God has come alive in my life. God has been faithful to me. God has kept His promises.

Quite often gifts come in packages we least expect. I can remember the first gift God gave me on this journey was the gift of peace. I did not recognize it at first. It was an unexpected package. Have you ever had an "unexpected gift?" Sometimes, the gift within the wrapping of the paper is bigger and better than we had imagined. Sometimes, the gift under the paper is different than we had expected. My husband gave me one of those "unexpected gifts" when he proposed to me on Christmas Eve, December 24, 1990. It was around 10:00 pm that particular evening. Bill had intended to surprise me and spent "hours" on planning the perfect "presentation". We were at my parent's home that evening. Bill, making sure we were alone in the family room, "set" the stage. He turned on the Christmas tree lights, and turned off the over head lights. My "place of honor" was thoughtfully picked. Then, bending down on one knee, Bill orchestrated his plan. "Anne I have been waiting for this moment for a long time" he began. As he handed me a beautifully wrapped package that resembled a tiny jewelry box, my heart began to race. I *knew* it was an engagement ring! We had discussed plans on getting married, and I had suspicions that he might propose to me on Christmas. In fact, I was *quite* confident that this WAS Bill's plan...so confident, in fact, that I told several friends! However, to my humble surprise, the box contained a pair of earrings...stunning earrings no doubt, but truly not what I had anticipated! This was the first unexpected present! Bill must have seen the look of disappointment on my face, and questioned whether or not I liked them.   I did...how could I not? They were eloquent and dazzling. It was just not what I had expected.

As I reflect on this moment, I realize that my plan is not God's plan. How often do I become overly confident that my plan is perfectly aligned with His plan? I am often arrogant in thinking that my plan, my way, is better than God's. I often suggest my ideas to the Creator of the universe, thinking that perhaps He never thought of that quite like I had! Again and again, God gently reminds me that His ways are BEST. I need to trust Him. All the time, in all of my ways!

Next, while still on one knee, Bill gave me my second gift. I was still thinking about the earrings and how they were supposed to be an engagement ring. I opened up the beautiful package wrapped in Christmas paper. It was a gorgeous music box. This musical decor was a square turquoise box, outlined with gold. I opened it up to hear it play The Wedding March. It did not matter though; I could not hear it. My disappointment made me deaf! As a matter of fact, my disappointment was so loud that I did not hear <u>The Wedding March</u>! It could have played <u>Mary Had A Little Lamb!</u> I missed the moment...again. While Bill was working hard to coordinate his plan, I was caught up in my own self pity. I was thinking "How am I going to tell all of my friends that there was no ring?"

Finally, last but not least, Bill gave me a third gift. This box resembled the first jewelry box, only it was wrapped in gold paper. I slowly unwrapped his gift. My excitement had melted away. Could this be a matching necklace? As I opened the box, my jaw fell to the ground! Yes, inside the small jewelry box was my engagement ring! WOW! Bill proposed as he said "Anne, will you marry me?" With tears in my eyes, and a smile on my face, I said "yes". Bill had worked incredibly hard to plan this moment. He wanted it to be perfect, but I got in the way! I had expected only a ring, but I received much more. His preparations were planned with every detail in mind. Bill started with the smallest gift, and attempted to set the stage with the music box. His planning and coordination took hours of energy. He wanted it to be perfect! I was so eager and sure of the ring that I missed the beauty of the unexpected...and the unexpected became the finest gift of all!

As odd as it may seem, the day I was diagnosed with breast cancer became the beginning of a journey in which unexpected gifts became abundant. This voyage came in a package I least anticipated. The package was not wrapped in pretty paper. The gift did not glitter with the holiday lights of the season. The journey was tough. However, God planned surprises for me along the way. He orchestrated peace for the journey. There were moments that I felt that surely, my way would be better. There were moments that reminded me to stop and look at the gift at hand. I am learning to enjoy the beauty of the unexpected. God provided the support for every moment that I needed it. I began to trust His ways. Sometimes the path became clear as the beauty of the moments unfolded. This was hard for me because I often want to know the plan days prior to its unveiling. Instead, I have learned to trust that the "engagement ring" is there. The gifts leading up to that moment are part of the beautiful plan. I need to trust that God is EVER present. I need to trust that His plan is better, MUCH better than mine. I am humbled by God's love for me. I have felt His peace, amidst the storm.

My storm was forecasted on November 30th, 2007. The call came at 5:15pm to be exact. My OBGYN called me at home to inform me that I had Stage 2 breast cancer. I was sitting on my bed, breathless.

"Anne, it does not look good" she began.

My doctor continued by apologizing for being the start of the Christmas season.

She apologized for my future.

She apologized because I am a wife.

She apologized because I am the mother of three young children.

Little did I know, this journey became a gift, wrapped in the disguise of cancer. The fear, the unknown, the doubt, the questions, and the future have caused me to lean on God unlike any other experience I have known to date. He did not let me down. He did not let me go. May this book remind you of God's love, His compassion, and His omnipotent presence.

The story begins when I went for a routine mammogram on November 13th, 2007. The technician found something "suspicious" and I was called back for an ultrasound on November 19, 2007. On November 29th, I had a biopsy, and those results indicated I had a Stage 2b tumor in my right breast. Generally speaking, doctors define breast cancer by stages. Stage I is usually when the tumor is 2 cm or smaller. Stage 2 is a tumor size bigger than 2 cm but less than 5 cm. Stage 3 indicates a tumor size greater than 5 cm. Stage 4 indicates the cancer is any size and has spread to the chest wall or the skin (Breast Cancer, Treatment Guidelines for Patients, 2006).

My initial response was "This cannot be happening!" I asked my doctor if this is fatal. She quietly replied "Probably not." I was overcome with fear as I sat on our bed, hung up the phone, and sobbed in Bill's arms. He was amazing. Bill was strong, yet compassionate. He was with me every step of the way. My husband's words of wisdom came at the perfect moments. He believed in me, encouraged me, and supported me.

I will never forget the fear. It paralyzed my body, increased my heart rate, and made my spirit quiver. The moments to follow were filled with phone calls and prayer requests. The world of technology made the news of my breast cancer spread like wildfire. My children did not know, but I am sure that deep down inside, they were questioning their mother's "odd" behavior. That evening a dinner had been planned with my extended family. They drove in from Cincinnati Ohio to join in the weekend festivities to celebrate my father's 70th birthday. The weekend was to begin with dinner at a local pizza parlor. I truly did NOT want to go. I was just getting accustomed to the words "I have cancer" when I was expected to go to a pizza party. I was scared. In looking back, I remember my fear being "real", yet not viable. Perhaps I feared as if this new diagnosis made a "mark" on me. I was scarred. Would my family still love me, despite the cancer? My cousins quickly heard the news. Their very first response was to embrace me. This embrace was worth more than a thousand dollars because it brought our relationship to a deeper level. It brought a new eloquence. Their embrace was delicate, yet firm. It spoke a million words, words of hope, encouragement and strength. Their embrace spoke volumes...yet not one word was uttered. It was truly powerful. I am glad I had found the courage to go. Hind sight reminds me that the ugly face of fear can often be trampled by the gift of courage. It was all part of "The Plan."

After a restless night's sleep, I woke up early the next morning. Bill was already awake. God, being the faithful God He is, planted a song in my heart that morning. This song, The Voice of Truth, became my mantra. It is sung by a contemporary Christian group named Casting Crowns (2003). The chorus is written:

"The Voice of Truth tells me a different story.

The Voice of Truth says do not be afraid.

The Voice of Truth says this is for My glory.

Out of all the voices calling after me, I will choose to listen and

Believe the Voice of Truth."

The song's lyrics depict two stories of biblical figures that faced fear and conquered! They were triumph amidst the storm because they kept their focus on God.   The song reminds me that the storms can be big, but...God is ALWAYS bigger.

The first verse in The Voice of Truth sings of the battle between a shepherd boy and a giant. It is the story of David and Goliath. The account is told in the first book of Samuel, chapter 17. Envision with me, the Philistines setting up camp as they were gathering for war. Meanwhile, the Israelites had assembled a camp in the Valley, and drew their battle lines to meet the Philistines. The Philistines occupied one hill and the Israelites the other.

Goliath, representing the Philistines, was a nine foot tall giant. He wore a bronze helmet on his head and a coat of armor around his body. As if his size was not threatening enough, Goliath carried a spear for a weapon. Goliath challenged the Israelites to find a "suitable match". The Israelites, in turn, choose a shepherd boy…yes, a shepherd *boy* named David to defend them. (1 Samuel 17:32). Why would anyone do such a thing? Choosing David, a shepherd boy, to fight Goliath, a giant? Perhaps it was because David was confident…not in himself, but in the power of a *living* God. David announced "The Lord who delivered me from the paw of the lion and the paw of the bear will deliver me from the hand of *this* Philistine" (1 Samuel 17: 37). WOW…what confidence David had in His God! When it was time, David took his staff, chose five smooth stones, put them in his pouch, and with his sling in his hand, approached the enemy line. The battle began. David, approaching the Giant Philistine said to him "You come against me with sword and spear and javelin, but I come against you in the name of the Lord Almighty, the God of the armies of Israel, whom you have defied." (1 Samuel 17: 45). As the Philistine moved closer to attack him, David reached into his bag, took out a stone, slung it and struck the Philistine on the forehead. The giant fell face down on the ground, and died! David, a shepherd boy, triumphed over the giant with only a sling and a stone.   (1 Samuel 17:48-50). WOW...did you read that? Read it again. David, a shepherd boy, triumphed over the giant with only a sling and a stone. The underdog won! The bad guys lost! The boy triumphed over the giant! God did the unthinkable! Amazing! David, a *boy*, fought Goliath, a *giant*, and won! David was sure of His God, confident of His deliverance. David trusted God. David listened to the voice of truth. He listened to the voice that said "do not be afraid". He chose NOT to listen to the voice of fear, the voice of doubt, the voice of the enemy, but instead, David listened to the voice of his God. David knew of God's faithfulness. David believed that God is a vital and living presence in his life.

The same is true today. Here we are, thousands of years later, and our God continues to be a faithful God. God is a vital and living presence in our life. He cares about you; thinks about you, and defends you, no matter how big or small feel that you may be. Call on His name. Believe in His love. When life throws you a curve ball, need to listen to the voice of truth. Fear may know our name; doubt may make us turn our head. Be strong! Take courage!

Despite *all* of the voices this world is calling you, remember to stop, and listen to the voice of truth.

"The Voice of Truth tells me a different story.

The Voice of Truth says do not be afraid.

The Voice of Truth says this is for My glory.

Out of all the voices calling after me, I will choose

to listen and believe the Voice of Truth."

The second lyric of this song sings about Jesus' disciple, Peter. In the gospel of Matthew chapter 14, it is written that after Jesus fed five thousand people with five loaves of bread and two fish. Jesus dismissed the crowd, and before going to the mountainside to pray, he instructed his disciples to get into a boat and go to the other side of the lake. (Matthew 14: 23). Meanwhile, as the disciples were far from the shore, a storm moved in. (Matthew 14: 24). I can only try to imagine what it must have been like. Envision with me…being inside a boat, in the middle of a lake during a bad storm. Now visualize the waves, hear the wind, and feel the rain on your skin. Imagine the fear when a man approached by walking on the water! WOW!

We will pick up the story in Matthew 14, 24-26. "During the fourth watch, Jesus went to them, walking on the lake. When the disciples saw him walking on the lake, they were terrified "It's a ghost they said, and cried out in fear". It is written: "Jesus reassured them by saying "Take courage! It is I. Do not be afraid!" (Matthew 14: 27) Jesus' response? REASSURANCE! When we are scared and frightened to the core of our being, what does Jesus tell us to do? Be REASSURED! Have faith. Be confident. Be free of worry. Have no anxiety.

Peter, on the other hand, was unsure. He tested the truth; questioned authority and asked the impossible. "Lord, if it **is** you, tell me to come to you on the water" (Matthew 14: 28). Jesus simply said "Come" (Matthew 14:29).

When I think of Jesus inviting Peter to walk on the water, despite the storm, I imagine the courage it must have taken for Peter to take that first step. Peter questioned Christ, asking Him to prove that He was who He said He was. Peter's belief in a true living God was solidified when he stepped out of his comfort zone, and onto the water.

How many times do we question the unbelievable? How many times do we question God's authority? How often do we think the possible is impossible?

Jesus simply calls your name and invites you to "Come". Do you have the courage to go? Peter found courage. He got out of the boat, and began walking on the water! The unbelievable became believable because he listened to the voice of his Savior.

But then it happened...Peter's center of attention switched to the rainstorm. His heart shifted from focusing on His Savior to looking at the storm. It was then that he began to sink. The story unfolds:

"When Peter saw the WIND (emphasis mine), he was afraid and beginning to sink, cried out 'Lord save me!' Immediately Jesus reached out His hand and caught him. 'You of little faith' he said 'why did you doubt?'" (Matthew 14:30-31).

Did you notice that when Peter focused on God, he was able to walk on water? When Peter focused on the storm, he began to sink. Reflecting on this passage, I realize that when I focus on God, my courage strengthens. When I focus on the "storm", I begin to sink. My heart was engulfed in fear quite often on this journey. When those moments consumed my heart, I found my husband, and simply asked him to sing to me. Bill would start singing the chorus from this song, and my fear subsided, my panic dissipated. God's voice of truth settled my heart.

"The Voice of Truth tells me a different story.

The Voice of Truth says do not be afraid.

The Voice of Truth says this is for My glory.

Out of all the voices calling after me, I will choose

to listen and believe the Voice of Truth."

This song became my mantra. The song helped me to focus on God, not on the storm. The Voice of Truth tells us not to be afraid! When those voices of self doubt; those voices of fear; those voices of self pity flood your heart, STOP. LISTEN. God invites us to come, to follow Him. God promises peace to His people. God's plans are better than our plans and His ways are better than our ways. Let your confidence be rooted in God and may you find the courage to step on the water when He invites you to come. Believe the unbelievable. The journey is unforgettable.

~Two~

Strength For The Journey

"God is our refuge and our strength, an ever-present help in trouble."
(Psalm 46:1)

I have often heard the phrase *"It takes a community to raise a child."* I think it also takes a community to love someone through the darkest of times. The weekend following my diagnosis was surrounded by friends, family, phone calls, and prayers. Their support truly reflected God's provisions of being ever-present. Through my community, God has shown me His promises of refuge and strength in my time of trouble. There are many moments I will never forget. My extended family supported me and my church community fed me. My work community embraced me. This chapter will reveal God's presence on my journey through the ministry of our community. His love is quite unbelievable!

One of the first phone calls I received was from younger brother, Don. He told me two very important things. First, Don reminded me of my heritage. The unforgettable phone conversation began with

"Anne, remember you are your father's daughter."

My father, Karl, is a strong man. At the age of 22, my father came over from Germany. Not knowing the English language, my father got a job as a carpenter. He married the love of his life, and had three children. My sister Lisa is 15 months older than I am, and my brother Don is 4 years younger. Being a man of few words, my father's actions often spoke volumes of his love for us. His dedication to his family is his highest priority. My father has a strong work ethic. He often worked sixty plus hours a week in order to support our family. Yet, he *never* complained. When reflecting on my childhood, I remember thinking how deeply my father loves us. He always put his family first. He worked hard and sacrificed his own personal desires in order that we might have a good life...never once complaining. My brother's encouraging words that Friday evening reminded me of the rich heritage running through my veins. I learned about hard work from my father. His gift would be a source of strength for my journey.

One of my most favorite moments with my father occurred on May 9, 1992, my wedding day. I was at my parent's home prior to the wedding. After getting dressed, family pictures were taken.

It was then time to go to the church. I could not find my father. My mother informed me Dad was in the backyard. Moments later, I found him sweeping acorns off the patio...in his tuxedo! It was time to go to church and my dad was doing yard work! As I approached, I saw tears in his eyes. When I asked him if he was ok, my father put down the broom, and hugged me. Choked by emotion, he could not bring himself to say the words "I love you Anne." He did not need to say anything...the tears in his eyes spoke volumes of the depth of his love for me. I will never forget that embrace. It was strong, yet gentle; powerful yet soft. It was as if I was empowered and cradled within the same moment. No words, just an embrace...an unforgettable embrace. It was as if I was cradled under God's wing.

Over the past several years, my father has faced many health challenges. He has climbed these mountains with grace and courage. My father has diabetes. He is a liver transplant recipient. In 2004, my father was diagnosed with Burkette's lymphoma, a fast spreading form of cancer. The oncologist told him to put his life in order, as he had 4-5 months to live. That was seven years ago, and my father is still living! He is truly a pillar of strength and a symbol of hope. Throughout it all, I have NEVER heard my father complain. He is not a quitter. My father is strong. Throughout my own journey, my father inquires about others, never drawing attention to his own needs. So you see, when I was diagnosed with breast cancer, my brother's encouraging words reminded me of the rich heritage running through my veins. I learned about hard work from my father. His gift would be a source of strength for my journey. His strength is part of my blueprint. His heritage is my heritage. Don's phone call reminded me that this rich lineage is part of my DNA. His statement was truly quite powerful.

The second important thing that Don told me was

"Anne, I love you."

I could not remember the last time my younger brother told me he loved me. It not only brought tears to my eyes, but hope to my heart. His love was renewing and refreshing. His words were powerful and unforgettable. I often think that we are afraid to tell our family and friends that we love them. We miss those opportunities to encourage and empower. Words have the power to replace loneliness with love. Choose your words wisely.

Many other people within my family and community carried me throughout the journey. My sister's love was reflected through phone calls and cards. Lisa spent many hours in prayer for me. Her presence at the foot of the cross brought me encouragement. It empowered me to take another step when I felt like giving up. She reminded me to take my vitamins and drink plenty of water! Her love for me is compassionate and sincere.

And then there is my mother...I mean my own personal *angel*. My mother is amazing! She walked the journey with me, through thick and thin, never letting go of my hand. I will never forget hanging up the phone with my doctor that Friday evening. I cried in my husband's arms. Then I called my mom. She is my INCREDIBLE cheerleader! She knew what to do. She knew the words that were encouraging. She cried with me, laughed with me, held my hand and cradled my heart. My mother was there when we met with the surgeon. My mother was present to my husband when I was in surgery. She was there to watch my children when I needed a nap. She did my laundry. My angel shopped for us. She sent me cards in the mail...always at the right moment in time. I never know how she did that. She even found a Hallmark card about losing hair during chemotherapy! My mom sat through *EVERY* chemotherapy treatment with me. She listened to me when I complained. She hugged me when I cried. She comforted me in my fear. My mom sent me flowers on the day I was diagnosed *AND* on the day I finished my last treatment of radiation. She gave me hope, vacuumed my house, and held my hand. My angel listened to me when I told her how God was working in my life. She listened when I was afraid God forgot about me. She went wig shopping with me...and out to lunch when I was brave enough not to wear my wig. She didn't care...angels usually don't.

On Wednesday, December 5th, 2007, Bill, my mom and I met with the surgeon. Dr. Schuh was astounding. Her knowledge complimented her graceful bed-side manner. She did not rush our appointment. The first piece of information she told us was that my tumor was not as big as first indicated...only 1 cm! This put me in a Stage 1 classification...NOT stage 2b! Whew...what a relief! A lumpectomy was scheduled for the following week. The surgery would be outpatient.

Up until this point in time, we had not told our children about my cancer. Bill and I had decided to tell our three children after our appointment with

Dr. Schuh. We had wanted to obtain as much information as possible in order to answer any questions that might arise. After prayerful consideration, Bill and I called a family meeting. As we sat with our children around the kitchen table, I said a prayer to ease my trembling heart. I know that God promises to be our refuge and strength, an ever present help in trouble. God truly showed up as I began. The words came out easier than expected.

"Mommy has breast cancer".

I continued by explaining I was going to have surgery to remove the tumor and then undergo treatment to prevent the cancer from coming back. Erik (9 years old at that time) asked a lot of questions. Paul (age 8) was quiet and Emily (age 5) played as she sat on my lap. Erik wanted to know details. Erik wanted to know what causes cancer. Erik wanted to know if boys get breast cancer. Erik wanted to know if I was going to die. I responded

"Someday, somehow...but not now and not by this!"

His last question was "Why you Mom?" He wanted to know why I, his mother, got breast cancer. I took a deep breath, looked at Bill, and replied:

"I don't know why me, but, if we trust in God on this journey, and people watch us trust God amidst the storm...what do you think might happen?"

It was then that Paul spoke up for the first time. In his honest innocence, he said

"People might learn to love Jesus more."

WOW...they *are* incredible...aren't they? I count this as a blessing.

On December 11, 2007, I had a lumpectomy. I was really nervous the night before. My best girlfriend and my mother came over to share some words of encouragement, but there was still such a void in my heart. It was an emptiness; a nervousness that I could not pinpoint. Unsure of this feeling, I asked God to settle my spirit. At that moment, there was a knock at the door. My cousin Peggy, a recent breast cancer survivor, came to visit me. She had just started her chemotherapy treatments, and was one step ahead of me on the journey! Her doctor is Dr. Schuh...my doctor! Peggy came over to give a hug, and offer some heartening words. Little did she know, she filled the empty spot within my heart. Her words of support were the answers for the "unknowns" that my heart was anxious about. Sometimes a little hope from someone who has walked the journey before you can be *THE* exact encouraging word you need. Peggy was ever-present for me. God used her to be strength for me! Her visit was a gift I will never forget. God answered my prayer. Count another blessing.

"God is our refuge and strength, an ever-present help in trouble."
(Psalm 46:1)

The Christmas of 2007 was special in its' own unique way. My energy was low, and I fought the anxiety of what might be lurking in the New Year ahead. Decorations were minimized. I do not remember shopping, and the spirit of Christmas was hard to find. Despite this, people showered their love upon our family. A friend of mine gave me an Amaryllis flower. It bloomed in our family room, a tall brilliant red flower! Within the restlessness of my home, a flower bloomed. My spirit was dry, but the flower's fragrant beauty renewed me. It was a dazzling reminder of God's presence in my life. This same friend took opportunities to love me through this desert time. She would often send gifts anonymously. On any given day, a package would arrive in the mail. One week she sent me seven decorative holiday mittens...one a day, filled with goodies for the kids (chocolate, holiday pencils, candy, etc.). The mittens have words of encouragement stitched on them...words like love, peace, joy, and hope. Initially, we did not know who these presents were from until the end of my journey. We just knew God loved us through the storm. The kids had fun guessing who these surprises might be from. We called her our Christmas "angel". I now hang the mittens up on my mantle at Christmas, as they have become part of our permanent holiday decorations. The mittens will always remind us of God's presence on our journey. We still talk about our angel's gifts and the way God orchestrates His love for us through the people in our lives. His face radiates when we look for Him. Count another blessing.

"God is our refuge and strength, an ever-present help in trouble."
(Psalm 46:1)

Unforgettable gifts were in abundance this holiday season. One dear friend gave me a Mizzou baseball cap...complete with lights that illuminate the darkness. I will FOREVER be grateful that someone was already thinking of ways to keep my soon-to-be-bald head warm in the upcoming winter! Count another blessing.

Another gift came through a cohort at work. She organized a "pink bracelet campaign". I work with disabled children as an itinerant occupational therapist in a school district within the area. I am assigned to three different school buildings. My friend organized a "pink bracelet campaign." She sold lots of pink bracelets to co-workers. In turn, my co-workers wore the pink bracelets as a sign of hope and encouragement. I felt the support of others throughout my day. Peers would wear these pink bracelets daily. My hope was manifested just by seeing the pink bracelets. There was a unified power among us. Words could not have spoken as loudly as the optimism brought from these bracelets.

Another Christmas gift came as a surprise. Every year the Hoffman family draws names for a gift exchange. This year, my sister-in-law thought it would be nice if we did something different in lieu of gifts. Her directions instructed us to donate money to a charity that would honor the person whose name we drew. On Christmas day, after eating a delicious meal, we sat around the fireplace for the "gift" exchange. We had to identify who our secret pal was and to what organization we donated money to in their honor. This was such a great idea! It amazed me that there were no duplicate charities. The stories behind the thoughts of these "gifts" brought tears to my eyes. Soon, I discovered that this sister-in-law had my name. I thought that for sure a donation would be made to the Susan G. Kormen breast cancer foundation. To me, it was obvious that my breast cancer had consumed my life, as well as the lives of those I love. I thought that others saw "CANCER" when they thought of me. How could they not? Boy, was I wrong! Instead, she honored me and my life. She looked beyond my illness and wanted to donate to an organization that reflected my talents, and my life, not my disease! Thinking of the life I bring working as a pediatric occupational therapist, this friend donated money to the St. Louis Children's hospital! She told me that she wanted sick kids to get healthy in my name! It was such a holy moment for me. Her gift was more than a monetary donation. It was a reminder that cancer does not define me. She looks at me with love and respect. She honored who I was. She honored my being, not my disease. She made me feel whole. She loved me through the eyes of my Savior. When God thinks of us, He thinks about who we are, and the person He created us to be. His love honors us. God sees beyond the surface, beyond our illness, beyond the shortcomings,

beyond the bald heads and our sinful hearts.
Count another blessing!

"God is our refuge and strength, an ever-present help in trouble."
(Psalm 46:1)

After surgery, I met with my team of doctors. The team included a radiation oncologist (Dr. Beat) as well as a medical oncologist (Dr. Stutz). I met with Dr. Beat on December 26 and with Dr. Stutz on January 8. They were both puzzled with my "numbers". The course of treatment was not as black and white as one might expect. My tumor numbers invited the team to discern and discuss the most optimal course of treatment in order to prevent recurrence. Typically, chemotherapy is the course of treatment for people whose tumors are larger than 1 cm. My tumor was 1.1cm by .08 cm. Physicians grade tumors by how much they look like normal cells. Grade 1 means that the cancer cells look like normal cells. Grade 3 cancer cells do not look like normal cells. A cancer's grade, along with its stage, is used to determine treatment (Breast Cancer, Treatment Guidelines for Patients, p. 84). Chemotherapy is considered for women who have grade 3 tumors...not on grade 1. Mine was grade 2! The team then looked at the kg factor. If the kg factor is high, chemotherapy is prescribed. If the kg factor is low, chemotherapy is not given. Guess what...mine was at 50%!!! The team then suggested sending my tumor to a lab in California that could identify the "make-up" of its tissue. This would help in deciding if chemotherapy would be beneficial in reducing my chances for recurrence. We thought that this test would surely be the deciding factor! However, those results came back indecisive as well. I was truly on the fence! After much thought, prayer, and discernment, I decided to do chemotherapy as well as radiation in order to reduce my chances for recurrence. The team told me that these treatments would decrease my chance of recurrence by 7-8%. Bill and I thought that it was well worth the trade-off. Once again, Bill and I called a family meeting. When explaining the decision to our children, it was Erik, once again, that asked all the questions.

I will never forget his deep yet simple response.

 "Mom" he said, *"Why wouldn't you have chemotherapy?"*

I replied, *""I will lose my hair Erik."*

He responded, *"You will still be my mom, right?"*

I smiled and said, "*Yes*".

He smiled and said, "*Then what is the big deal?*"

Count another blessing.

"God is our refuge and strength, an ever-present help in trouble."
(Psalm 46:1)

With that, I agreed to a regime of four rounds of chemotherapy, 33 radiation treatments, and five years of taking a prescription medication called Tamoxifin. I wanted to start my chemotherapy treatment as soon as possible! I figured that the earlier I started this regiment, the quicker I could complete it. I just wanted to get it over with! It seemed as if my first appointment would never arrive. My team of doctors needed to "meet" in order to verify that this particular course of treatment was the best for me. However, one doctor went out of town. Another doctor worked only part time. Two weeks passed and still no plans were set. I became restless, asking God to help expedite the process. After all, I thought I knew what was best for me. My patience wore thin, and my prayer became a plea. Finally, on Tuesday afternoon, January 15th, 2008, I received the phone call that chemotherapy would begin the very next day, Wednesday, January 16th, 2008.

I will never forget that day. As an itinerant occupational therapist, I travel between three different schools. Every Wednesday, for the past decade, I have worked at Sherwood Elementary, located in Arnold, Missouri. It just so happened that January 16th was a Wednesday. My chemotherapy was scheduled to begin at 10:00 am, and I had contemplated whether I should even go to work for a little while, or should I just take the whole day off. I decided to go to work in order to wrap up a few loose ends prior to my appointment. I figured it would keep my mind off things, as well as help the time pass. I entered the school office at 8:00 am, said "hello" to the secretary, and proceeded to check my mail.

Moments later, I noticed a teacher wearing a pink sweatshirt. (Anything pink catches my eye. I notice pink ribbons, pink mailboxes, pink slippers, etc. It became the "color of the year". My children became good at pointing out the pink breast ribbon logo whenever they found one.) Here I was inside Sherwood's school office, noticing this pink sweatshirt when a speech therapist entered the office. She was wearing a pink sweat shirt as well.

She asked if I had noticed the shirts. I replied "Yes, but I didn't get the dress code memo for the day." She continued by asking if I *REALLY* noticed the sweatshirts. Printed in the top left corner of the sweatshirt were the words *"Sherwood Cares"* followed by the pink breast ribbon logo. Within a moment's time, I realized that the sweatshirts were for me! *EVERY* teacher in the building wore a pink sweatshirt that day! As I walked through the hallway of Sherwood Elementary, I was overwhelmed with love, support, and tears. Everywhere I looked, I saw pink sweatshirts. Classrooms on my right had teachers with pink sweatshirts. Classrooms on my left had teachers with pink sweatshirts. The cafeteria workers wore pink sweatshirts. Cohorts from the therapy department wore pink sweatshirts. By the time I got to the therapy room, I was one big tear drop! Waiting for me in the therapy room were the principal and kindergarten grade teachers. They gave me the gift of my own pink sweatshirt. The entire staff wore pink sweatshirts in my honor! Their support reflected God's strength and ever present help. Their efforts to support me allowed God to transform me. Their "yes" became a pillar of strength that will not be broken. God planted a thought within the mind of a kindergarten teacher, and acting upon it, allowed her to be the reflection of His face in my little world. How powerful her "yes" became!

After wiping away my tears, the principal asked,

"When do you begin chemotherapy?"

I replied, *"In 2 hours!"*

The best part of the story was that the staff did NOT know that chemotherapy was beginning that day. They only knew that it was Wednesday, the day that Anne comes for Occupational Therapy. The staff planned to wear the shirts on Wednesday because it was the day I was there! It was also my first day of treatment. God perfectly planned it that way! I am humbled to say I was the one who tried to interfere with His plan, pleading for "my terms", "my will be done", not His. I was impatient and wanted to start chemotherapy days prior to January 16th. But this was not God's plan. I would have missed this "divine appointment" if my will were done instead of His. I continue to learn life's lessons about trust, lessons about His will being better than mine, lessons about letting go and letting God, lessons about His promises.

On the way to chemotherapy that first day, I had an unforgettable inner strength that I received because of someone else's "yes". I will never forget that empowerment. I will never forget His embrace. I will never forget His presence in time of trouble. God is my refuge. Staff members continue to wear their pink sweatshirts on Wednesdays, years later! It has become a weekly reminder of God's promise. He will never let us go! Count another blessing...no, count two!

I now challenge you. Be that empowerment for someone. Trust in God's plan. Look for Him. Lean on His strength. Encourage one another and build each other up. Your "yes" can be a transforming and empowering event in someone else's life. What a difference you can make!

That January morning I called my husband to share my story. He in turn, told his friend about this incredible gesture of love. Her response was simply

"Well, would you look at Jesus!"

Yes...would you look at Jesus!

~Three~

Hair Today, Gone Tomorrow

"He has made everything beautiful in His name."
(Ecclesiastes 3:11)

When I first received the diagnosis of breast cancer, I remember thinking

"I do not care if I lose my breast; I do not care if I lose my hair;
I just do not want to lose my life!"

After my lumpectomy, and with chemotherapy lurking around the corner, I realized it *DID* matter if I lost my hair. My hair did not fall out over night. It was a process. ..I soon began to realize *EVERYTHING* is a process. I first noticed my hair thinning about seven days after my first chemotherapy treatment. Bill, who is personally familiar with this subject, always had an encouraging word to say. I can specifically remember the day I realized his balding head would have more hair than my head. With tears in my eyes, I looked at him and admitted my fear
 "You are going to have more hair than me!"
 He replied, "Yes, my love, that's true, but your hair *will* grow back Mine will not!" He always has such a great way of making me feel better!

"He has made everything beautiful in His name."
(Ecclesiastes 3:11)

"Vanity"…Webster defines vanity as "inflated pride in oneself or one's appearance" (Webster). I have never considered myself vain…until now that is. As I looked in the mirror, I remember thinking how sad I was when this "unimportant" thing called hair all of a sudden became so important! I was angry because it bothered me. I became irritated because I never thought my hair was a defining attribute of mine, until now. I wanted others to look at me and see me, not my cancer. I became annoyed because I feared that being bald would be an outward sign of the battlefield. My baldness was like a proclamation to the world, announcing the journey I was currently on. I began grieving my loss, and the person I saw when I looked in the mirror. I was accustomed to my style, my look, my hair. People knew who I was when they saw me. My hair was part of my identity. I remember wishing it was not so important, wishing it did not bother me. It didn't bother Becky. Becky is one of the most courageous women I know. She lost her hair when she underwent chemotherapy, yet choose to not wear her wig. She went out in public without anything on her beautiful bald head. My friend's confidence was solid, her strength

43

amazing, and her courage was powerful. As a preschool teacher, Becky went to work bald. She surrounded herself with children. Did they care? No! They saw the beauty within. I often remind my heart of this truth.

"He has made everything beautiful in His name."
(Ecclesiastes 3:11)

My oncologist advised me to buy a wig before my hair fell out. It offered an opportunity to purchase a hair piece that would match my color and style. With that in mind, my mother and I went wig shopping. I was scared the first time I stepped into a wig shop. The lady asked if she could help me, and I began to cry. Standing there, amongst shelves filled with hairpieces, knowing my hair would be replaced by one of these, was a very humbling experience. The fitting of a wig was not an easy task either. It was hard to get a good "fit" when I still had my own hair. The styles I tried on were different colors than the color of my hair. I had to "imagine" these wig styles in my hair color. Once a wig is chosen, it is then ordered in the desired color. Quite challenging! Five days and three wig shops later, success! I found a great wig...or should I say "cranial prosthesis". (The medical term for wig, often utilized for insurance reimbursement.) The process continued.

"He has made everything beautiful in His name."
(Ecclesiastes 3:11)

It was not long until my hair began falling out. I soon noticed more hair on my pillow and less on my head. My scalp itched, and hair fell out. I picked hair off of my shirts, wiped it off the countertops and piled it in the shower. Someone told me I would know when it was time to get it shaved off. She was right! That day came eleven days after my first chemotherapy treatment. The pile of hair in the shower that morning was huge. It just would not stop falling out! I had originally asked Bill to do the honors, but he humbly declined the offer. I mustered up some courage and made the inevitable phone call to my beautician, Sharon. She invited me to come to the shop after she finished with her last client that afternoon. So, with my wig in hand, I got into my car and drove to the shop. Sharon first cut my hair short, and then took out the razor. Using an eight gauge, my friend buzzed my hair. I can remember crying, watching my hair fall to the floor. I looked for internal beauty. I sure did not see it in the reflection I saw in the mirror. My defining moment came when I got home. With my wig on my head, I took a deep breath, and went inside. The first thing Bill said was

"You chickened out...didn't you? Your hair looks great!"

I LOVE THAT MAN!!! My best friend could not tell that I had a wig on! The tiny seed of confidence grew within my heart. My children could not believe it either. Paul responded with "Prove it Mom!" My self-assuredness sky-rocketed! I was beautiful to the most important people in my life, my family. God certainly was making everything beautiful in His name.

 This journey is such a process. Just when I think I took a step or two forward, I went two steps backwards. I wanted to sing all the way through the journey, but fell short. My wig soon became my "security blanket". I wore it in public, and would take it off at home. My family was instructed not to answer the door until I had my wig on. I wanted to "hide" imperfection.   I did not want friends or relatives to see the "real" me. It was easier to hide under the wig than to stand firm without it. How often do we hide behind those masks, afraid to let people see the real us?

I can remember a few short days after my beautician buzzed my hair. Sharon shaved my hair with an eight gauge razor, I still had hair...it was very short hair, but hair nonetheless. On this particular evening, my family just sat down for dinner. I will never forget how badly my head itched. I got up, found a wash cloth, stood over the trash can, and rubbed my itchy head. The wash cloth was now covered with my short tiny hair! I then realized that hair falls out no matter if it is long or short! I looked at Bill, with tears in my eyes, and said I want to be done with it! He stood up, smiled, and embraced me. Paul said "*I think Mom needs a group hug!*" The children got up and gave me the hug of a lifetime. There I was, my heart fragile and my head bald, standing in the middle of my kitchen, being completely surrounded by my husband and children, feeling like I was the most beautiful woman on earth! There is *NOTHING* like being loved by children. They love unconditionally, love without reservation, no strings attached...hair or no hair. True love is when walls are down, barriers are gone, and our hearts (and heads) are truly exposed. When I am at this spot, and people love me, I feel the depth of Christ's crucified love. This experience came through my children. I think that when God Himself told us to love as little children. THIS is what He was talking about. Once again, God was making everything beautiful in His name.

During the process of becoming familiar with the "new me," I found myself growing in unexpected ways that only God could have perfectly orchestrated. On the way to work one morning, I was listening to my favorite Christian radio station, JOY FM. I caught the tail end of a game typically played on Friday mornings. The contestant has to name as many things as they can in a given category within the allotted time frame of 15 seconds. On this particular morning, the category was "Name things that you wear on your head." The contestant named only 1 thing..."Hats". This led to an interesting talk show discussion. The focus of the conversation was naming things people wear on their heads. The two DJs identified other items like ear muffs, barrettes, ribbons, etc. I thought for a moment. I know a lot of things people wear on their heads...especially if they (me) are BALD!!! Then it happened. Before I knew what I was doing, I called into the station and provided information relevant to their conversation! I gave them a quick 60 second in-service on cranial prostheses, wigs, turbans, scarves and hats...that's right...ON THE AIR!! I did something I have NEVER done before! Courage became a gift my bald head gave to me! In turn, the DJs prayed with me and promised to remember me in their daily prayer. God's beauty radiates. The journey offers opportunities to practice the life lessons taught. Rely on the courage within, trust in the gift it brings you.

Sometimes you have to just roll with the punches. I am *sure* most breast cancer survivors have a "most embarrassing moment", or should I say I hope most survivors have embarrassing wig moments, because I do! Mine occurred at one of my radiation treatments.   This day was like any other ordinary radiation day. I arrived, signed in, and proceeded to the dressing room. I got a pink gown out of the dresser, and went to change clothes. The two changing rooms were already being used, so I went to the bathroom. Keeping my wig on, I took off my pull-over shirt, thinking that the shirt would fit over my wig. Well, I was wrong, it didn't. The wig came off and fell into the...you guessed it...*toilet*!! Thank goodness it didn't sink! I was mortified! I proceeded to pick my wet wig out of the toilet, shake it out and put in on, as if nothing ever happened.   I thanked God that I was not at home because chances are, there would have been other things besides water in that toilet bowl! (Those of you with boys in your household understand what I mean.) I checked the mirror and went for radiation, hoping no questions would be asked. I was not willing to confess. I was no worse for wear. The technicians were polite, but I am SURE that they were probably wondering what that funny smell was! Silly as it may sound, when I found the courage to laugh at myself, I found a hidden beauty...a beauty that made me want to smile.

On April 4, 2008, through God's grace, I finished chemotherapy. Of course my mother stood by my side...faithfully! My sister-in-law came to join the festivities. Then we celebrated! The wonderful nurses put a pink boa around my neck, a crown on my head, and blew bubbles as they took out the IV. It was a moment of strength, accomplishment, and courage. We extended the party over lunch, sharing life with friends. It is a strange feeling to be so proud of something accomplished that was never on a "goal" list. It was probably one of the hardest things I ever did, and to say "I did it" brings a smile to my face and courage to my heart. I claimed the victory over chemotherapy and found courage to wear a hat that day! Yes, wigless!! It was almost as if I wanted the world to know my victory. I felt different when I was losing my hair.

Then, it felt like chemotherapy had control. I wanted to hide under my wig. Now that it was over, my head (and the little hair on it) proclaimed that I was *NOT* defeated, and I was in control. THAT felt GREAT! The courage and strength came from God. Now I have conviction; I look at life with a new vision, and have an inner strength, an inner beauty. He truly has made everything beautiful in His name!

~Four~

Walking By Faith

"We rejoice in our sufferings because we know that sufferings produce perseverance; perseverance character, and character, hope. And hope does not disappoint us."
(Romans 5:3-5)

This gift of suffering came wrapped in a package that was not very attractive. This journey has brought me many opportunities to reflect on life, think about courage, and pursue ideational philosophical concepts such as suffering. Suffering is something that I do not fully understand. It puzzles me. When my heart tries to comprehend the logic behind the pain, I become confused. I cannot discern what God wills or what God plans. The core of my being believes that God is good, all the time, God is good. Psalm 119 verse 68 proclaims that "God is good and what He does is good." I then ask myself, if this is true, why does suffering exist?

Sometimes I think that suffering is a direct result of our actions. We are given the gift of free will. God does not control us. Our independent choices can lead to suffering. For example, when I eat too much, I gain weight. If I choose to smoke, my consequence may be the development of lung cancer. Perhaps suffering is the result of poor life style decisions. The possibility of suffering increases if I decide to spend all of my money on gambling. It may cost me my job, my family and/or home. Emptiness, anguish, and affliction may be the penalty of these decisions. This, I can understand. However, it is those situations when there is no logical explanation for suffering that I do not comprehend. I think about the child who has leukemia. What about the unexpected car accident that took the life of a husband and father of three? I will always question the existence of disease, and unfortunate circumstances. I think about those people who have committed suicide, leaving family members and loved ones in a state of grief. I often wonder why great women in my life are unable to have children. Their desire to love a new born into life runs deep within their soul. The unthinkable becomes indescribable.

When my heart takes me to those places where my mind cannot comprehend, I need to remind myself that God is God and I am not. I cannot explain the reasons for suffering, or why it exists. BUT, I can rely on what I *know*. I *know* that God our Father is familiar with suffering. God knows the meaning of a broken heart, because His heart has been broken. He sent His only son to carry out a mission, knowing exactly how the mission would end. God watched as His own flesh and blood was betrayed, scourged, and crucified. I cannot imagine the anguish God felt as His very own Son hung on a cross to die. God, the Creator of the universe, wrote the definition of suffering. He understands our pain when as it pierces the heart. Our Father's love for us is larger, wider, and bigger than the deep pain of His own suffering. God would rather suffer to be with us, than to live without us. God, the All Powerful, the Alpha and the Omega, the Almighty One, our Constancy, our Hope, our Salvation, knows what it is like to suffer. I know He understands the pain in my heart when I am suffering. He embraces me and reminds me that He will never, ever leave me. This brings comfort to me when I face the trials of life. Knowing that I do not have to understand the reasons why suffering takes place, I just have to know I will not be alone. This, in and of itself, brings comfort to my weary soul. God understands my suffering, and He promises never to leave me.

I have come to acknowledge God's promises because He has made them known to me. His word is truth. The Bible speaks of His promises. His promises are real. I know because I have experienced how His holy words have jumped off the page and embraced my soul. I felt His love, have embraced His hand, and felt His strength. I **know** of God's promises:

~God promises to never leave us or forsake us (Deuteronomy 31: 6). No matter what, He is present. Seek Him.

~God promises us that He will be our strength, our fortress (Psalm 18:2). When you are weak, He is strong. Ask Him to put you on His shoulders.

~God promises to always love us because His love endures forever   (1 Chronicles 16:34). You belong to Him, embrace His love.

~God promises that His grace is sufficient for us, and His power is made perfect in weakness (2 Corinthians 12: 9). God gives us the grace we need to endure. His power is glorified, and His face made known. Look for His grace, grasp it, and never let go.

~God promises perfect peace for those whose minds are steadfast in Him (Isaiah 26: 3). Think about God, pursue Him, seek His ways, and He will give you "perfect peace".

I promise!

My suffering has taught me that God is a keeper of His promises. In fact, God's outpouring of love for me and my family was quite overwhelming. My sister-in-law came over, gave up her day, and cleaned our house. For *six* months people brought us food. These people were friends and family within our community. Parents from our children's soccer teams prepared meals. Friends from our church community made food. Scouting parents signed up for meal preparations. The mother of one of Erik's friends organized meals from his classmates! WOW!!

Initially it was very hard to for me to receive this tremendous outpouring of love. You see, I am a much better giver than receiver. The suffering brought a role reversal to my life. Bill reminded me that by receiving, I was giving others the opportunity to be Christ. Humbly, I allowed people to serve me. Open-handed, I learned to receive.

When reflecting on my journey, I often recall the story of the paralytic that Luke writes about in his gospel. In Luke chapter 5, verse 17, Jesus is found teaching the leaders of the nearby villages. Men from Galilee, Judea, and Jerusalem were gathered around Christ to listen to His word. Verses 18-19 reads:

"Some men came carrying a paralytic on a mat and tried to take him into the house to lay him before Jesus. When they could not find a way to do this because of the crowd, they went up on the roof and lowered him on his mat through the tiles into the middle of the crowd, right in front of Jesus." (The New International Study Bible)

I imagine my community, carrying me on a mat, finding any way possible to bring me to the throne. When fear surrounded my heart, I would receive a card in the mail. When I lost hope, a friend would call. When I was hungry, food would show up on my doorstep. When I was tired, opportunities for naps seemed to magically appear. When I was down-and-out, someone was lifting me up in prayer. My friends and family brought me to the throne. Christ was truly present within my community. Their attention, love and generosity were genuine. I could see Christ in their smile, hear Him in their voice and feel Him within their embrace. This has been the single most humbling experience of my life. I will never forget it.

Luke's account of the paralyzed man continues in verse 25 of Chapter 5. Christ's healing power is revealed. When people come together for a common cause, and present the cause to Christ, great things happen. I think that God often uses these opportunities for His glory.

"He (Jesus) said to the paralyzed man, "I tell you, get up, take your mat and go home. Immediately he stood up in front of them, took what he had been lying on and went home praising God." (The New International Study Bible)

My friends and family brought me before the King's throne. My community had come to be my servant.

They were Christ for me. God's grace humbled me. I let them be my servant, and in doing so, I was healed. I will forever praise His holy name.

These experiences have taught me about the ways of our God. I have learned that God is good; *ALL* the time God is good! Our world is a broken world. Its order is often confusing. Morals are distorted, hearts are broken and lives are in disarray. Despite the brokenness, the TRUTH remains that God is good. *All* the time, God is good. God is good when I have breast cancer, and God is good when I am healthy. How do I know? Experience! Experience has been my teacher and life has become my classroom. It is within its boundaries that I have learned about God and His provisions.

~I have learned that nothing changes God's goodness.

~I have learned that our God is powerful.

~I have learned of God's deep love for us.

~I have learned that God never leaves us. I understand His constant presence.

~I have learned that God will guide us if we allow Him to.

~I have learned that God never lets go... God *never* lets go. His face is always near.

~I have learned that God's way is perfect, the promise of the Lord is true (Psalm 18:30).

As I wrap up another chapter, I am not any closer to unlocking the secrets of suffering or the reasons for its existence. However, I am closer to understanding the perseverance that has been brought forth from this gift of suffering. My character has been polished because of its presence. My hope has been renewed. It has truly become a gift, wrapped in a package I had not recognized.

~Five~

The Acorn

"Blessed is the man who trusts in the Lord, Whose confidence is in Him. He will be like a tree planted by the water that sends out its roots by the stream. It does not fear when heat comes; its leaves are always green. It has no worries in a year of drought and never fails to bear fruit."
(Jeremiah 17:7-8)

It was one week before Christmas when a simple question led to a profound impact on my life. Two weeks after my lumpectomy, Erik, our nine year old son, found an acorn in the front yard. Bringing it in, he asked me,

"If I plant this, will it grow?"

I responded, "Sure", but thought what do I know about planting acorns? Despite my fatigue, I attempted to remain optimistic in order to suffice my son's curiosity. Erik proceeded to go to the garage looking for a pot and some dirt. He then independently planted the acorn and placed his masterpiece on our living room end table. He kept his pot of dirt under a lamp 24/7. Erik watered his acorn daily. I was amazed at how my child became responsible for this acorn, yet, he does not always remember to put his shoes away! It was as if his faithfulness to this acorn had some direct relationship to God's faithfulness to me. Erik tended to the acorn. Erik watered the acorn. Erik made sure the acorn was always under the light. His tender loving care fostered a sense of responsibility and hope.

The New Year brought in its own set of challenges...chemotherapy was not on my list of New Year's resolutions. I felt buried by the weight of it all. However, every week as I would dust around this pot of dirt in my living room, I wondered about the acorn. The winter lingered. My hair began to fall out. Every week I looked in the mirror at my bald head. The weight of my journey was heavy. Every week I would dust around the acorn. I often wondered if the acorn felt the weight of the dirt. It appeared as if the acorn was not growing. There was no visible sign of life. For me, I wondered if chemotherapy was working, for it felt as if it was stripping me of my personal being...it did not "feel" healthy. I needed to remind myself that these drugs were actually healing me, despite the side effects. No hair, no sprout. It never seemed to bother Erik though. He was faithful. He watered his acorn every day, despite no sprout. Every day he continued to love me, despite my bald head! The lamp stayed on 24/7. The acorn remained under the light. I was reminded that I needed to stay "under the SON light". Erik believed in the hope of the acorn. Erik believed in the hope for a cure. Erik's faithfulness is a gift I will always treasure.

As January melted away, February came and went. No sprout. Soon it was March. No sprout. Erik did not give up. Daily, Erik watered. Weekly, I dusted around the pot of dirt. April brought spring and the start of radiation. My journey was making me weary. Not Erik though. He remained faithful. He remained hopeful. His actions were encouraging. He did not forget. Erik watered the acorn daily. He never gave up!

I finally asked a cohort if she knew anything about planting acorns. She said that acorns were really hard to grow. She informed me that October is the best month for planting. Further information indicated that when planting an acorn, the tip has to be pointed down, several inches below the dirt. I am not sure if Erik did any of these specifics, as my guidance lacked the wisdom needed to properly plant an acorn. It made me wonder about the pot of dirt in our living room. I questioned the hope. I feared the worst. I wanted to give up. Radiation was becoming exhausting. I went everyday for 6 ½ weeks. The outward fruits of my labor were blisters on my skin and marks on my breast. As the weight of the journey became heavier, I wanted to give up. I can remember telling my husband that I was finished. I told him that I thought 3 ½ weeks of radiation was plenty. I told him *"I think I am through"*. He just smiled, looked at me, and replied *"No you are not."* I responded and said "I am tired. My blisters hurt. My skin is burnt. Why should I go on? Give me one good reason, just one."

"You're alive...that's why."

I gently lowered my head and said "Oh...good point."

Erik is his father's son. He never questioned the journey of the acorn. He never asked why it took so long to sprout. He just believed. Despite any outward sign of life, Erik continued to care for the acorn, without complaint. I leaned on my son's strength when I wanted to give up. I borrowed some of his hope when mine was running low.

Then it happened! About two weeks and ten radiation treatments later...the acorn sprouted!

Our family cheered as if we had just won the lottery! UNBELIEVABLE!! WOW!!! This green bud brought with it new life! The tiny little sprout gave me the strength and courage to complete my radiation treatments.

On May 15th, 2008, I finished my last radiation treatment. I will never forget that day. Before leaving for work that morning, my husband gave me a card. He said he has been *waiting* for this moment. I opened up the envelope, pulled out the card and read the words "THE OAK TREE". WOW... my husband found a Hallmark card about an oak tree! With tears in my eyes, I read:

The Oak Tree

A mighty wind blew night and day.

It stole the oak tree's leaves away,

Then snapped its boughs and pulled its bark

Until the oak was tired and stark.

But still the oak tree held its ground

While other trees fell all around.

The weary wind gave up and spoke,

"How can you still be standing, Oak?"

The oak tree said, "I know that you

Can break each branch of mine in two,

Carry each leaf away, shake my limbs,

And make me sway.

But I have roots stretched in the earth,

Growing stronger since my birth.

Through them, for you see, they are the deepest

Part of me.

Until today, I wasn't sure of just how much I could endure.

But now I've found, with thanks to you,

I'M STRONGER THAN I EVER KNEW.

(Hallmark)

Bill wrote a message inside that reflected my strength in the journey. He reflected on my inner strength. We talked about watching our grandchildren run around the oak tree, while listening to their father tell them the story of the acorn.

Today, our oak tree is about eight inches tall and is on our porch. My treatments are over and I have a full head of hair. Erik continues to care for his tree. It is a   constant reminder of the power of hope, the grace of God, and the story of a miracle. God is good, ALL the time, God is good. God is faithful, EVEN when the weight of the world is heavy. His grace is amazing and His presence is unbelievable. When fear creeps its ugly head into my heart, my God's voice, the voice of truth, calms my soul. God used an acorn and the heart of a nine year old child to teach me about His faithfulness. My roots run deep and my core is strong. I just never knew how strong until that storm came!

~Six~

Heaven Bound

People will watch our response to life's adversity. What will they see? Will they see our fear or will they see God's glory?
(Bill Hoffman)

The concordance explains that the "heart" refers to the center of one's being, including mind, will and emotions (p. 1475). On this cancer journey I have thought about life, and about death. It is not so much that I am fearful of death. Instead, I can honestly say I am afraid of leaving my family. Who would be my husband's soul mate? Who would take care of my children? Who would remember their PE clothes? Their lunch money? Doctors appointments? Who would tuck them in at night? There were plenty of days that my mind was scattered, my spirit was fearful, and my will was weak. On these days, Bill reminded me that people will watch my response to this misfortune. People watch adversity. It is how we react to our hardship that speaks volumes of our character and how we live our lives. During hard times, I need to decide what I want people to see. Do I want them to see my fear or do I want to reflect God's glory?

Twelve years ago my husband and I conceived our first son. Despite many complications, I carried him for four months. I had a "subchorionic" bleed. The

bleed was from my uterus, located below the outermost sac that surrounded our child. 1% of pregnant women have this condition, and 90% of this 1% are able to carry full term. I remember the day of the ultrasound. It was my mother's birthday, March 26th, 1997. The doctor told me that despite the bleed, my baby had a vital heartbeat, and the baby's growth corresponded to his gestational age. He recommended that I go home, put up my feet and take it easy. He said that I would either "pass" the bleed or my body would reabsorb it. Chances were I was going to have a healthy baby boy. Several hours later, the pain became severe. While at home, ~ 6:00 pm, I passed the placenta, thinking I had passed "the bleed". Twenty minutes later, in my bathroom, I gave birth to our son. Wow! He was the size of my hand, from my fingertips to my wrist. He was clean and beautiful. Our baby had ten fingers and ten toes. He had fuzz for hair, and his fingers were crossed, lying on his chest. I laid him on the counter, and called my husband. We wept.
Bill was great. He made the necessary phone calls to the doctor and funeral parlor. In the state of Missouri, a doctor has to pronounce someone dead prior to the funeral parlor accepting the body. So, we wrapped him up, named him John, and I held him as Bill drove us to the hospital. It was there that the physician pronounced him. The funeral parlor was then able proceed with the arrangements. He explained that "most parents

just discard the fetus in a container". Bill reassured the doctor that he was not to throw away our son! The physician then had called labor and delivery in order to verify protocol. Jan, a friend of ours, was the nurse working in *Labor and Delivery* that evening. She answered the phone, not yet knowing that John was our baby. It would be just like God to orchestrate a friend of ours to work behind the scenes that night! A week later I saw Jan. She told me what an inspiration our baby was. It was then that I found out she was the nurse working in *Labor and Delivery* that night. She explained that John made a "pro-life" statement, just by his existence! Nurses and staff members were in awe by his tiny being. John's presence spoke volumes about the lives of unborn babies. Jan hugged me as I wept.

How will we respond to adversity?
Will people see us our will they see God's glory?

On the way home that evening, I called my mother to wish her a happy birthday. Between my tears, I apologized for miscarrying her grandson on this, her special day. My mother's response is one I will *never* forget. She simply said

"Anne, no one has ever given me an angel before on my birthday!"

My mother's response reminded me of God's goodness at a moment when my heart was shattered.

On March 26, 1998, exactly one year later, God blessed us again. I was admitted to that same hospital, preparing to give birth to our second child, Erik. He was born March 27, 1998. It was exactly one year and one day after John's birthday, and a day after my mother's birthday. He was full term, healthy and beautiful. God's glory revealed once again!

People are watching...what will they see? Will our hearts be pure? Will they be able to see His presence radiate within the core of our lives or will fear and doubt emanate? How will our response to life's difficulties reflect our fear OR His glory? Remember, people are watching.

Last weekend the phone rang. Bill answered. As he handed the phone to me, I certainly did not expect the conversation that was about to occur. This phone call was unlike any other phone call I have ever received. It is one that I will never forget. On the other end of the receiver was our dentist. Our dentist has never called me at home. All necessary scheduling was conducted through his secretary. I was surprised to hear his voice, and soon realized that this phone call was a "blessing" for me, but a "necessity" for him. I was grateful for his phone call, for his gift of his time, his energy and his honesty. To think that he took a moment to call me was truly special. Let me explain. Our dentist was currently undergoing treatment for cancer. A month prior, he sent us a letter explaining that he had decided to discontinue his dentistry practice. This kind gentleman was diagnosed with the same cancer that stole the lives of his mother and sister. His letter explained that when the steadiness of his hands began to affect his work, he decided to call it quits. Now, a month later, I found myself in the middle of a conversation that revealed his prognosis. His doctors gave him only six months to live. Our dentist called me to provide the details of his plan for the rest of his life. He explained that the lease on his office needed to be breeched. He elucidated that the medical bills cut his savings in half. He cried when he spoke of the sadness his wife was experiencing. He planned to pack up and move to Colorado, to be with his son, so his wife would not have to be alone after he died.   He called me to say thanks for being a part of his life.   He called me to tell me what an honor it was to be my dentist. He called me to remind me of how good God is, that this journey gifted him with a deeper understanding of our Savior's love for him. WOW! It was quite unbelievable that my dentist was sharing his relationship with Jesus with me! I could hardly take it all in! We talked about the past, the present and future.   We ended the conversation with "good-byes". However, his good-bye was a true good-bye. It was a *until we meet again in another time and another place good-bye."* I know I will probably never talk with him or see him again, at least until that other time and place. Despite the finality of his "good-bye", his words were peaceful and kind. The certainty of his death was inevitable, yet, he did not seem to be afraid. His voice was calm and without quiver. His strength was powerful. His courage was amazing. I truly saw God's glory in the middle of a heartbreaking situation.

"People will watch our response to life's adversity. What will they see? Will they see our fear or will they see God's glory?

Three days later I received another phone call. My best girlfriend's mother passed away. She had battled with lung cancer for eight months. I missed the opportunity to say good-bye to her. She was in ICU during the last few days of her life. I lived the journey of her final days through my friend. I tried, best as I could, to hold her hand along the way. I was impressed by the evidence of God's grace and presence during this trying time. The beauty of it is exemplified in my friend's realization of God's presence during this most difficult time. Like my dentist, she understands the truth of God's love for her. She humbled herself at the cross, knowing she is unworthy of our King's love, yet received His love as a gift, freely given to her. She believed! My friend's belief in this truth sustained her when the grip of death was taking away her mother's last breath. I am proud to know her. I am blessed to call her my friend. I am humbled by her faith.

On September 2, 2010, my friend Patti died from breast cancer. Her husband and children were present as angels escorted her from this life to heaven. Her death saddened my heart unlike anyone else I knew. Perhaps it was because she was my friend. Perhaps it was because she had the same disease I had. Perhaps it was because she left behind her husband and four children...my biggest fear. The disease that took her life also was a part of my life. I watched my friend live with hope, and die with courage. I watched her radiate God's glory. I prayed with her, clinging to God's grace, while begging Him for miracles. Our relationship planted its roots in grade school, and deepened in high school. Her parents continue to be a rich part of our parish, and incredible pillars of faith in our community. My friend reflects the faith that her parents have taught her. Our lives parted after high school and reconnected within the parish boundaries were we grew up. When I learned of her breast cancer, I put my name on the list to provide meals for her family. A year later, being diagnosed with breast cancer myself, she made my family dinner.

"People will watch our response to life's adversity. What will they see? Will they see our fear or will they see God's glory?

Reflecting back on these events that have shaped my life, I cannot help but think about life and death. I often think about our son John. I think about how God's hand carried us through the trial. I think about the finality of my relationship with our dentist. He took the opportunity to reach out, to risk, to say good-bye. I will never forget his courage. I think about the finality of my relationship with my friend's mother. The journey was not easy. My friend embraced the cross. In doing so, she found the strength she needed to expose God's glory. My friend reacted to the adversity in her life with grace. People were watching. I think about the way my friend took an ugly disease and used it to bring beauty to her corner of the world. She smiled when she felt like crying. She listened to me talk about the trials of "back to school shopping", when I realized she wished it was her buying paper and pencils alongside the 100s of other shoppers at Wal-mart. She never complained about the pain I saw it her eyes. She did not want to talk about the cancer. She wanted to talk about life, about how God was working. This courageous woman truly lived in the glory of our Creator. I will never forget the beautiful way she lived her life.

I think about my own mortality. How do I want to live? Life has no guarantees. I am learning that I must daily jump on the opportunities as they present themselves. Every day I am flooded with opportunities to say a kind word, do a nice deed, to call a friend. Every day I am called to humble myself before the cross, knowing I am unworthy of our King's love, yet receive His love as a gift. The truth of His love is empowering. His grace brings me the courage to act upon the opportunities that come my way. It was my husband who once told me that people will watch our response to life's adversity. What will they see? Will they see fear or will they see God's glory? I have seen God's glory shine within the hardship of life...and how beautiful it is!

~Seven~

God's Perfect Paradoxes

"For I know the plans I have for you," declares the Lord, "plans to prosper you, and not to harm you, plans to give you a hope and a future."
(Jeremiah 29, 11)

Recently my friend told me about a funeral she attended. She caught my attention as she began to talk about her neighbor's memorial service. Embedded in the eulogy was a story about a lady who fell off a cliff. As she was whirling through the air, she caught sight of a tree branch that extended from the rock. Reaching out, she grabbed it and hung on tight, clinging for dear life. The lady looked down, fearful of letting go. She was a long way from the ground below. The lady prayed "Dear God, will You help me?"

God replied "Do you trust me?"

The lady's response "Yes, I trust you."

God answered: "Then let go."

Since then, I have thought about my level of trust in God. How much do I really truly trust the Master of the Universe? I try to listen for God's voice when I pray. I wait for Him to answer my prayer. Sometimes I find that His response is completely opposite of what I wanted or thought I needed. I have found myself hanging onto a branch for dear life, when God is asking me to let go. He softly whispers "Do you trust me?" Hesitantly I say "Yes" and let go. I know that when I trust Him, He reveals Himself. God's way is better than mine. God's answer to prayer comes with my "active" participation. Faith is letting go when we cannot see the ground beneath us. God's paradox.

At times, God's philosophy appears illogical. For example, His Majesty, the Alpha and the Omega, the Savior of the world, sent His only son to be born of a young virgin named Mary. She was an unmarried, humble girl, without a noble name, without riches, without earthly extravagance. I would have thought that Creator of the Universe should at least have had earthly parents that were from a wealthy royal lineage. It just makes sense. Instead, God's own Son was born in a manager, a stinky stable, amongst cows, donkeys, and sheep. The smells of the stable do not appear to be the perfect atmosphere for a King. His bed was a feeding trough, filled with itchy, scratchy straw. Where was the castle? The royal bedding? The fresh linen? The warmth of the Inn? The sweet smells Majesty deserved? Instead, of a palace, our Savior was born in a poor, dirty corner of the world.   Why? Love. Our King stepped off of His throne to stoop to the depth of our existence to display His perfect love. Another amazingly perfect paradox!

Christ's life and teachings are filled with paradoxes that depict our Almighty's frame of reference. This philosophy is often opposite from what makes worldly sense. His ways are perfect, our ways are not. His teachings are life giving. The Bible is filled with the paradoxes of God. For example,

- ~"Love your enemies and pray for those who persecute you" (Matthew 5:44)

- "He who finds their life will lose it, and those who lose their life for my sake will find it." (Matthew 10:39)

- "Whoever becomes humble like this child is the greatest in the kingdom of heaven." (Matthew 18:4)

- "If anyone wants to be first, he must be very last, and the servant of all." (Mark 9:35)

- ~Love your enemies, do good to those who hate you, bless those who curse you, pray for those who mistreat you. "(Luke 6:27-28)

- "If anyone strikes you on the cheek, turn to him the other also. If someone takes your cloak, do not stop him from taking your tunic." (Luke 6:29)

- "If anyone would come after me, he must deny himself and take up his cross daily and follow me. For whoever wants to save their life will lose it, and whoever loses their life for me will save it."(Luke 9: 23-24)

These commands appear opposite of how the world teaches us to be. The world teaches us to live with a "me first" philosophy. Not God. His love is the biggest example of extreme love, a love that does not make sense. God loved us so much that He sent His own son to be crucified for us. Christ's death was ugly...uglier than one could ever imagine. Our Savior was whipped, scourged, and beaten. He was laughed at, mocked; hit, kicked, and spat upon. Our Redeemer wore a crown of thorns. He carried His own heavy cross. Nails pierced His hands and feet. He hung on the cross to die, because He loves us. Christ came into the world, not as a prestigious nobleman. Rather, he humbled Himself in order to meet us in our brokenness. Christ, in His greatness, became man in order to embrace the wounds of the people He loves. We are treated like royalty, and God paid the price. God stepped off of His throne and placed Himself beneath us. Why? LOVE. What a paradox!

This journey has made me reflect on God's goodness. His grace has been truly sufficient for the voyage. I look back on the gift of this journey and I am grateful for the blessings it bestowed. If given the option, I would not have chosen this road. But as I sit on the other side, I am grateful for having had the opportunity to travel on it. Sometimes I think that I understand the perplexity of the whole thing, only to realize God has a lot more to teach me. May you be blessed with ALL of the gifts God has planned for you. May you receive these gifts with eyes that are focused on Him. May your spirit be open to trust God's ways. Lean not on your own understanding, but engage in the promise that He knows the plans He has for you. Plans to prosper, not perish. Plans to live and not die.

As I bring this book to a close, I believe that the journey of my breast cancer has truly been a gift. Perhaps if one would look at it through the eyes of the world, it may not appear to be as such. By reflecting through the eyes of our Father, it is truly a journey that reveals His deep, deep love for me. He carries me under His wing. I want to thank you for sharing the journey with me. May God reveal His promises to you, and forever hold you in the palm of His hand.

Blessings,

Anne Hoffman, Survivor

Notes

Chapter One:

1. <u>The Voice of Truth</u> ~ Casting Crowns (2003)

2. *The Holy Bible*, New International Study Bible ~ Copyright 1973, 1978, 1984, Zondervan Publishing, Grand Rapids, Michigan 49530, USA

3. Breast Cancer, Treatment Guidelines for Patients ~2006

Chapter Two:

1. *The Holy Bible*, New International Study Bible ~ Copyright 1973, 1978, 1984, Zondervan Publishing, Grand Rapids, Michigan 49530, USA

2. Breast Cancer, Treatment Guidelines for Patients ~2006

Chapter Three:

1. *The Holy Bible*, New International Study Bible ~ Copyright 1973, 1978, 1984, Zondervan Publishing, Grand Rapids, Michigan 49530, USA

2. Webster (Online)

Chapter Four:

1. *The Holy Bible*, New International Study Bible ~ Copyright 1973, 1978, 1984, Zondervan Publishing, Grand Rapids, Michigan 49530, USA

Chapter Five:

1. *The Holy Bible*, New International Study Bible ~ Copyright 1973, 1978, 1984, Zondervan Publishing, Grand Rapids, Michigan 49530, USA

2. Hallmark Licensing, Inc., Hallmark Cards, Inc., Kansas City, Mo 64141

   Toronto, Canada M21 1PG, Made in the USA

Chapter Six:

1. *The Holy Bible*, New International Study Bible ~ Copyright 1973, 1978, 1984, Zondervan Publishing, Grand Rapids, Michigan 49530, USA

Chapter Seven:

1. *The Holy Bible*, New International Study Bible ~ Copyright 1973, 1978, 1984, Zondervan Publishing, Grand Rapids, Michigan 49530, USA

Made in the USA
Monee, IL
05 December 2022